POIEMA
The Masterpiece

by

Nathaniel E. Quimada

By Nathaniel E. Quimada

ISBN:
Hardbound-978-621-8397-38-5
MOBI/KINDLE-978-621-8397-39-2
Softbound/Paperback-978-621-8397-40-8

Author: Nathaniel E. Quimada
Email: nathanielquimada@gmail.com
Contact No.: +639174506894
Facebook: facebook.com/nathaniel225
Instagram: @nathanielquimada
Twitter: @nathanquimada

Cover design by Ralph Enzo B. Rabaya

Published by:

Poetry Planet Book Publishing House
Rosario Pozorrubio, Pangasinan, Philippines
Contact Number: +639554960094
Email: maritesritumalta@gmail.com

TABLE OF CONTENTS

To my Mama Helen, Papa Carding, Kuya Gaylord, Ate Gay May, Manghud Ricardo and Rayver, Ate Ilonah, and Kuya Ian, my nieces and nephew, Quia, Zeal, and Zatrionah, you are all my inspiration. I love you all!

Acknowledgment

I would like to express my gratitude to my family for providing me with the strength and happiness that I require daily. Additionally, I would like to extend my appreciation to my colleagues at the University of Science and Technology of Southern Philippines (USTP) for their encouragement in my pursuit of writing this book. Furthermore, I am grateful to my close friends at my workplace for instilling in me the courage and motivation to continue. To my best friends, I am thankful for inspiring me with your life and unwavering support. I would also like to acknowledge SK Poblacion and Poblacion Barangay Council of Municipality of Claveria for their financial assistance towards this project. The people whose stories are featured in some of these poems and writings also deserve recognition for their contributions. Lastly, I am grateful to our living God for His guidance, wisdom, knowledge, and grace.

"For we are God's masterpiece. He has created us anew in Christ Jesus, so we can do the good things he planned for us long ago."

Ephesians 2:10 (NLT)

POIEMA
The Masterpiece

When I was young, I often heard from many people that reading English works and books would help us learn more, build our knowledge base, apply our analytical skills, stimulate our memories, and even expand our creativity. I made an effort, but it was challenging for me to comprehend every word I read. I concluded there that reading is not something I am interested in. When I was in high school, our teacher spoke to me in class, but I couldn't react since I couldn't understand what she was saying. My seatmate helped me grasp what our teacher meant by translating it into our dialect while my classmates laughed at me. I then learned how essential it is to comprehend the fundamentals of the English language.

I started asking my teachers for advice after I learned that it was still possible to master the fundamentals. Reading poetry works will help, according to her. Even though I had no interest in poetry, I started reading short stories and basic poems when I felt the need. I tried to make one and started writing a poem entitled *Be an Inspiration* in 2007. It was overly simplistic and had a lot of flaws and grammatical errors, but I was happy at the time since it showed that I could write in English. Even if reading is not my cup of tea, I am thankful that even a modest knowledge of poetry helped to fuel my desire to be a poet—or, should I say, a frustrated poet. It turns out that I co
and let the readers
and line of my works.

I admit that I am not really good at English, often times I am corrected by my "grammar nazi" friends, people who compulsively criticize or correct people's grammar mistakes, typos, misspellings, and other errors in speech or writing. But I acknowledge that I am not perfect and these pedants around me couldn't bring someone's passions down. I know my limitations and my capacity too.

After ten years, I produced several poems and other creative works, all of which were kept in my green notebook. The poems I wrote there were straightforward and not particularly poetic, but they were all based on my experiences, mixed feelings, and expressions of both struggle and triumph. Regrettably, I lost the green notebook. I was upset and reacted in a frantic way. Everything was written entirely by hand, without any copies, and not published; all were raw works. I lost my love of writing during that time, my desire to express something through writing.

Another years passed, and something awakened my desire to write again. I experienced a mental breakdown, a period of intense emotional distress. I felt that I was hopeless, I was unable to concentrate, had disorganized thoughts, and had changes in sleeping and eating habits. God impressed me with something to write, to write, to express something through writing. After completing a two-line poem, I feel relieved, so I continue writing from that point.

Great things await, do not bother to question yourself. Great things await; I should not bother to question myself.

With that lines, I survived.

Take a journey

Welcome to my poetic world! *Poiema*, my first published book, I sincerely hope you enjoy reading the assortment of writings I have put together. I write about many different genres, feelings, and experiences. I welcome you to peruse my words and discover what calls to you, whether it be the thought-provoking, the encouraging, the touching, or the humorous. I make an effort to provide you with a glimpse into my own personal journey and the experiences of the people around who shared their sentiments and testimonies, as well as to help you see the world from various angles. I have faith that you willfp discover something that resonates with your own particular experiences and that the poetic beauty of language will bring you joy and solace. I appreciate you taking the time to glance through my poetry collections.

It is my joy to create emotions and makes you write your own definition of every piece in your heart, so even if you can't feel the emotion I felt while writing these pieces or understand the meaning of each line, each word, each expression, remember that it is your understanding, your takeaway, your assumptions, and your perspective that for me matters.

Poetry is more than what's written on the page and what's meant by the words. Poetry is like stargazing; the constellations already exist, but it is up to the readers to give them form, meaning, and narrative. One thing is certain, though: the poet is aware of everything that exists. When you understand that reading this book is a conversation between you and me, you will understand the significance of each page. Poetry is a masterpiece too.

When I wrote this book,
I am with my mind and heart,
And my happy soul.

Raining Arrows

I stare at the map and a compass in my hand
I got the keys and the chest box where I stand
I am the prince of the kingdom and the heir of the land
And wait, I am confused, and I can't understand

I cry and stare up at the sky, and the prince is lost; I can't deny
I see raining arrows, and I hold my breath seems I am about to die
I see raining arrows, now I am excited, and I'm on high
I cry and stare up at the sky, I shout, and people don't reply

Again, I stare at the map, but I don't know what's my direction
I still have the key, but I lost the connection
I am now a slave of my past, my present, and scared of rejection
And now my heart sinks, living with a heavy heart with a question

Do I need to catch the rain arrows tomorrow?

This is some serious stuff. The weight of the world has become too much for this friend, and his mental health is suffering as a result. He needs help finding his way and is confused and disoriented. Let's help one another out, and we shouldn't turn our backs on those who are experiencing social isolation or condemnation. Give those who need someone to talk to your time, and you'll be rewarded with a more beautiful life. Pray for them and spread messages of hope and love.

Canvas

Our life is our masterpiece, it is up to us
On how we paint our story.
It is up to us how we see the substances we have.
At the end of the day, All our accumulated stuff
It will be presented as our greatest piece of work.

Empty Cup

Born with a silver spoon in her mouth
Living in gold, treasure, and accounts in the black
Just pursue her passion for compassion
Tagged with wrong motive and intention
They say it is impeded by a game of throne
You smiled and composed yourself
Hands in the lap and tried to understand the rule
There you say you're in an empty cup,
I smiled and praised the way you responded
The spirit of a brave woman rises in you
You don't need to play the game,
We understand someone's battle
Someone's cup may already be full.
But you may have an empty cup,
Empty because you chose to pour,
An empty cup over the golden crown.

No matter how far we've come, how wealthy we are, and even how close we are to owning the entire world. We will remember that we are not perfect and that there are many things we do not understand. I admire humble people and recognize that they still have a lot to learn and do.

Reduce to Tears

The earth is so heavy for you
And you can't bear the weight.
Your mind is trapped in murky thoughts.
For you, you have no way out.
You smile, you laugh, you weep, you cry, and shout
How are you?
You said you're sad and mad.
I was moved and felt so uncomfortable.
And again you begin to smile, you laugh, you weep, you cry
And impossible for me not to reduce to tears.
You were trapped, you were hurt, and your soul is in despair
I can sense the misery, it is heavy for me
I can feel the anguish, the sorrow, the pain, the grief,
And again, you begin to smile, you laugh, you chuckle, and grin
How are you?
You said you're stabbed; at the same time you're glad.
I tapped your back and again, you began to cry and laugh.

Mental health is extremely important. I admire those who fight depression and those who serve as a support system for others. Allow yourself to be a light for those who are struggling or in trouble. Let us all work together to help one another. Behold, how good and pleasant it is when brothers dwell in unity.

Glimmer of Hope

Brazilian Firetrees silently lament,
As the wind moves through, they cry their hearts out
A sadness is carried by the breeze and pavement
covered in tears
And it makes you long for an April day

Shoes

You cry so much about how people are doing.
Yet you refuse to acknowledge your flaws.
I feel sorry for you because of your innocence.
I regret that you are unable to see it.
Your flaws, your imperfections
Your deficiencies and shortcomings
Put yourself in their shoes.
And you'll realize how rude and insulting you are.
Being insensitive to others reflects our own personality.
How do you deal with insecurity, inferiority, and rejection?
Keep your feet on the ground,
Take the shoes and wear them,
and please be aware that character matters.

The Art of Regret

It is heavy on my heart
Difficult for me to start
In the mirror, I see the sorrow, pain, and shame
The regret is reflected, and it shouts my name

The art of regret is hunting me
I hold my tears and scream to be free
To the art of regret that holds a guilt
A strong force that strongly-built

Let the art of regret continue to chase me
Until the remorse stops shuddering my serenity
I understand how important to look before I leap
When failing, the disappointment is so deep

I hope and pray that this art can be used to grow
To teach myself and others and let them know
That the art of regrets lies a chance
To let go, to start, to grow, and enhance

Let the art of regret be a gift from God
To do what is good and to avoid what is bad

Stay with me

I hurt you oftentimes,
I heard you call me but I refused to listen
You reminded me of everything I need
But I denied following

Waves and storms smashed my way
I am hurt; I am in pain
Hey! Come and rescue me
I am trembling; I am down

Can you hear me? Listen!
Where are you? Don't forsake me
Promise I will hold on to your words
Stay, stay with me

Ecstasy

One, two, and three
It's really good to see you everyday
You're the only one for me
Two of us walking; how good to see
A three-word to say
I love you –
That's it, you're my ecstasy

A Part Of Me

Vastness of the universe in sight
Vague, bleak solitude at night
Eternal flames of burning desire
Ranging on like an unwavering fire
Yet no strength to move
Where my tears were not an objet trouvé
A part of me is confused,
A part of me diffused,
A part of me is abused,
A part of me is overused.
Everyone is celebrating apart from me.

Grasping at Straws

In difficult times, Oh God, I don't know what to do
My hope and joy fade away and are immediately
replaced by
fears and blue
Often times when I am desperate, I look up and call
you
But this time I can't hear nor see you, what shall I do?

Know that I am in dire straits
Give me a little hope for me to live, I will wait
Even when things don't go the way I want em to
I am certain you are here to carry me through

I am now grasping at straws
I know, my Lord my argument is for fools and against
the laws
When I know I can't save myself today
I beseech you to take me from drowning and keep me

Keep me as the apple of your eye, hear my prayers
and all these things,
and keep me hidden in the shadow of your wings
from the wicked who seek to destroy me,
and from my mortal enemies who surround me, I
pray
(Ps 17:8-7)

Sigh

It's as though time stands still, and the suffering growls that never ends.
It seems like the crying and howling never ends.
The ache in my chest makes it difficult for me to take deep breaths, huffing and puffing. Endless, intractable problems; friends and family who no longer appear to care; ears that seem deaf to my cries for help; the burden of believing that I am all alone flapping into my mind.

I don't know how many times I yelled out of sheer agony, but nobody appeared to pay attention, I groaned in despair but silence filled the air. No matter where I go, it seems like the darkness splatters and follows me. I've tried to follow the star's glimmer several times, but now I can't seem to find it.

I've lost the ability to see the sun and moon, and even the wind can't comfort me anymore, the rain no longer trickles on my skin. I don't think I'll feel any more pain if I strike myself with rocks again and over again.

Are my hopes completely misplaced? I can't even close my eyes without being overwhelmed by confusion, baffled at all times. Water no longer satisfies my thirst in the same way it always did. The burden of the things I'm carrying has rendered me helpless and unable to move on. Sigh.

I'm sure you'll understand if I ask you to let my weary soul rest. Allow my spirit even a brief respite. Just offer my troubled spirit a moment of solace. Please hear my pleadings, hear the cries of my anguished soul. Please. Plea... Plea... zzz...

....

Coffee Stains On My Paper

A cup of coffee on the table splattered on my paper
It's nearly midnight, I'm tired, and my body is screaming and worn
My favorite vanilla coffee ruined my late-night work.
The sip was enjoyable, but it eventually shattered my soul.

My hard work and energy consumption are now futile.
The coffee begins to leave its imprint.
I worked so hard that entire day and night.
And now my paper bears a coffee stain

My dedication, fortitude, and perseverance are about to be tested.
Even though it is only a piece of paper filled with pain and efforts
But my soul bemoans what happened, it freezes me, tell em!
I realized that I needed my work to take priority over my favorite cup of coffee.

Coffee makes us go – going where? I asked.
I took a deep breath, pondered and paused, and then took another sip.
I gripped the cup tightly and placed it on the safety spot
And I continue working over my tainted and stained paper

Cry One's Eyes Out

I'm engulfed with sorrow and tears like a sweeping storm
I am alone in the middle of the vastness of the ocean, where the pain is form
Have a lump in my throat and begin to hold back the tears
At that time, my only companion was despair and fears

Memories of the past keep on chasing my peace
My heart is bleak and miserable; help me to unload, please!
I can't move my feet, I tried to lift my hands as a sign that I need to endure.
But the burden became heavier, the agony is there, and a way out is obscure.

My heart sinks, broken, and it is too heavy
I don't deserve the pain I am in, and I envy
Take the grief and aches – I fall into pieces
And as time goes by, my anguish increases

The darkness of the shadow deepens
My body is little by little weakens
It's now too heavy for me and my body can't bare the load
The Lion of Judah, who conquered the grave, lead me to the right road!

The Lion hears my cry, and I find my strength anew
He lifted me high, guide my way, breaking through
I just found the rest I have been searching for so long
My soul rested, my yoke is now light and easy and made me strong

Let's all surrender our past, pains, and fears – there is a great Lion who sees our tears

Instead

I've tried talking to everyone here, but it seems like nobody's paying attention. I felt like I was drowning and could harldy take a breath. There were so many pieces of my heart, and they were being squashed so tightly, yet I couldn't do anything about it.

Instead of comfort and assistance, I was given worry and a wounded soul when I needed solace and assistance. I wondered if anyone cared if anyone would open their doors, so I started banging. I feel like giving up. The road ahead of me was wide and empty, and there was no sound in the air. It seemed to me that I had been forgotten about entirely. It seemed like nobody cared that I was in pain.

I pray you haven't had to endure such pain and suffering.

Nightmare, Mama

Ma, I should have listened to
I still remember the words you told me
Ma, I don't know why I still did it, and I am lost
I still remember the words you told me, mama

It's a nightmare, mama, and I hope it's just a nightmare
I want to wake up and hug you, nightmare, and it's a nightmare
Hear my cry but don't ask why
I am living in a shadow, mum

It's a mistake, and I can't explain
I learned from your words, and I pray to be okay
I will let your words be my guiding light
Mama, let your words be my shining light in my darkness

Sorry, if my nightmare hurts you so much
Ma, I know it's not just a nightmare
After this trouble and the consequences I encounter
Mama, let your words be my shining light, again

I know it's not just a nightmare, mama

I'm glad you've made it to this page and are still reading.
Play music that makes you feel good while you keep reading.
Every line's meaning is hidden in your soul.

Stage of Gold

To hear my name spoken by you fills me with dread.
In order to face those who actually care
Why my feet are shaking, I don't know.
The senses of those who have dispatched me
The gold stage frighten me
I've known for a few days now that I don't deserve
I have the gold, but I'm still plagued by shame.
Help me get up on stage
I assert that the words I have used are the words you have used.
I speak incoherently, with a lack of specificity and depth.
My soul cries out for strength to once again stand firmly.
While I'm here on the golden stage

Mum

You are truly one of God's most remarkable works of art;
I can see the incredible strength and beauty in your design.
Strengthened by your tears, I will not bow.
Taking on your perspiration has strengthened me.
To put it simply, I am the best version of myself
Because of the work, your hands did for me.

We are fortunate to have you as our mother
Since you are so strong and kind,
And you have helped us maintain a strong connection and bond
Distress, anguish, and difficulty block your path.
In spite of the challenges that life may throw at you,
You remain bold and persistent in your prayers for us.

Your love for us is unwavering.
Your wisdom, generosity, and kindness touch our hearts.
Despite the distance, I promise I am not far away.
God understands that you, through your prayers and hopes,
Our greatest source of strength.
The weight of the world may be too much for you to bear,

But you continue to hold on tight
In spite of the pain you experience from our embraces.
God must have known I would be frail even now,
So He created you that way.
Mom, you are so precious to me.
I praise God for the happiness you've brought to us.

You are the best -

Papa

What we imagine, what we hope for, and what we plan all stem from you.
I know you have many hopes and dreams for us
Because I see your struggles and your resolve.
Nonetheless, you feel bad that we can't accomplish this
Due to our resources and limitations.

You set the bar extremely high in terms of being tough and brave.
You may be able to hide your tears, pain, and prayers,
But I have no doubt that God hears and sees you.
For one, I take great pride in the fact that you are our father.

You have a hard time giving us what we need.
However, your eagerness and resolve to work with us is already an effort, and I pray to God that I may be an instrument in realizing your dreams.

Having you as a father is a decision we don't regret making.
Your flaws are God's way of reminding us that
Nothing is perfect in this world.
Despite this truth, I take comfort in knowing that God did create one thing perfectly—a father figures like you.

Thank you so much for being the greatest –

Empty Page

No matter how far we've come,
how wealthy we are, and even
how close we are to owning the entire world.

We should remember that we are not perfect and
that there are many things we do not understand.

I admire humble people and recognize that
they still have a lot to learn and do.

Admit

No matter how intelligent and talented we are,
let's keep in mind that we are still human and
are susceptible to making mistakes.

The secret to being perfect in this world
is never to be arrogant and pretentious.

Accept

I want to love you but can't because
I always know you won't.

I can't help but wish you happiness with others.

It hurts, but we must accept it because there are
things we know will make us happy,
but we must let go because we know it is not the right
thing to do.

To Keep Going

I had convinced myself that it would never happen to me again.
All this suffering, grief, and worry.
With you in my life, I have no desire to explore other options.
My previous belief that losing you was impossible was because we are so emotionally invested in each other, and your heart seems to be in sync with mine.
I am content with spending the rest of my life with you, and the concept of being without you has never crossed my mind.

I can feel your warmth and hear your heartbeat all the way here in my own bed.
I was kept alive by your speech.
Your heartbeat lulls me to sleep, and I can feel your body next to mine even when we are apart.
When you hug me, you make me feel safe and secure, and when you hold me tightly, your hands give me strength.

Never in a million years did I expect to feel this way very briefly.
Now that you've gone, I'm not sure if I'll be able to live through the pain, regrets, sadness, and breakdown or if I'll even thrive through them.
I hope my knees never give up on me, and I pray that God blesses me with an accepting mindset, clear reasoning, and inner calm.

God put you in my life for reasons: not only for me to be hurt but also to learn, cry, and overcome what life may bring. That's the path my life was always destined to take, and as difficult as that is to accept, I know you're a big part of the reason I'm able to keep going.

It's been a while since you are away from me. Your fragrance continues to occupy my thoughts, and the recollections associated with you remain enduringly vivid. I patiently await the opportune moment when I shall have the privilege to once again experience the tangible sensation of your skin, the tenderness of a kiss, the aroma of your hair, and the comfort of your embrace during moments of peace at night.

Despite the prevailing melancholy that envelops my nights subsequent to the moment you left, rendering my attempts at moving forward futile, a persistent dream takes refuge within me. It envisions a forthcoming juncture wherein you might reenter my life's sphere, not with the intent of becoming a significant presence therein, but rather as a harbinger of words and rationales that shall simplify the course of surrendering my affections for you, **to unshackle my heart,** love's tempest to fade.

Past

I'm content because you have someone to
spend time with and someone to lean on
during difficult times.

But keep in mind how contented
I was when I was still by your side,
when I was still your favorite,
and those times when you struggled to go
asleep without me.

Keep in mind that you once loved me as well.

If you've made it to this page in my book, you're
probably still having second thoughts about the
underlying
message of my poetry.

One thing, reread everything but don't follow any links.
Take pleasure in every word and line while sipping
a steaming cup of coffee or refreshing
fruit juice and sniffing every page.

A night

It's not uncommon for me to fall asleep
with nothing but a pillow for company.

The cushion soaks up my sobs,
and the only thing that comforts me is
the blanket's warmth.

Let's say you thought you were the
the only person I could trust at first.

Unfortunately, it seems as though
you have suddenly lost all of your memory.

Since I've been so frail recently,
I realized you might be just messing with me.

Silent

It's been a few days since I last saw or heard from you;
we can't communicate effectively via text.

Are you still interested in me? I wondered.

You didn't bother to wait for my calls
or answer my texts, so perhaps
you don't think much of me.

I pray that at some point in your life,
you will reflect on the time
you spent loving me so deeply.

Can I ask why it appears
I play no part in your life right now?

Siblings

I am grateful to my parents for the wonderful
upbringing
that they gave to my siblings and me.

I am relieved because they brought to our attention
the significance of getting along with one another as
siblings.

Now that I'm older, I can confidently say
that parents play a significant part in helping their
children
develop a healthy appreciation for their siblings
as they are growing up. I am who I am today also
because of them.

Look up

You, too, went through a variety
of storms throughout your life.

Your world will be shaken several
times as you experience raging seas
and enormous waves.

You are afraid of some things but continue
to hold fast and put your faith in God.

If you are in the midst of a storm in your life,
you must remain steadfast
and not give up because
God can calm down the storm once more.

Because of His great might and power,
He can calm you down despite
the difficulties you are going through.

Do not be afraid;
God is keeping watch over you.
He is aware of the challenges you face as well.

Valuable

Everything about our lives here is fleeting: our jobs, our homes, our possessions, even the prestige or power that keeps us going. Let's face the fact that everything we have today could be gone tomorrow, and instead of putting our energy into chasing material possessions at the expense of our eternal destiny, let's concentrate on finding meaning in life.

In the end, when our hearts stop beating, we can't take any of these material possessions to the afterlife; only our souls are genuinely valuable.

Even

Even though we know how bad we feel,
Even though they don't love us, we try to fit in with them.

We do it while we can because we are not yet tired.
The only thing we wait for is to be too tired to keep doing it.

Ponder

I find myself wondering if I am actually happy with what is happening in my own life, even while I make others happy and am a source of joy for others.

In the midst of all the care and consideration I provide to others, I can't help but ponder whether someone would take the time to recognize and take care of my own issues.

Let go

I want to love you but can't because
I always know you won't. I can't help but wish you happiness with others.

It hurts, but we must accept it
because there are things we know will make us happy,
but we must let go because we know it is not the right thing to do.

God has listened to my repeated prayers so that I could endure the heartbreak and sadness; for that, I am grateful. It's not easy, but I know that, like gold, **I have to go through it all to get to the beautiful end product.**

I still have a long way to go before I can let go of the pain, but I am able to go forward with some relief.

We must admit that it is difficult to move on; **moving on isn't easy.** It is hard because your typical routine with the person you love cannot happen at all. Not everything we desire is possible; we must all recognize that we must let go and admit that moving on is also a means of hurting ourselves.

It's important to remember that letting go isn't about causing more suffering; it's about finding relief.

Discover solace

Are you all right? Otherwise, engage in conversation with the kids or play with them. Feeling down? If so, dip your toes into the water.

Is envy plaguing you? If so, take a cup of coffee and a slice of cake. Are you feeling exhausted and ready to quit? Take a break, reflect, scream, and laugh!

Is a peaceful environment what you seek? Go to the seaside or a mountaintop to get some alone time. Are you looking for a way to lighten your sadness? Get in touch with the Supreme Being, take a note, and record your worries.

Do you need someone to chat with? Have conversations with random people. Feeling overwhelmed by anger? Sit and watch the sun go down while waiting for the nightfall.

Never forget that doing the unexpected can be a lifesaver and a path to self-discovery sometimes.

Undeniably, being **unable to love someone else** because your heart is still attached to the one who broke it is one of the worst feelings in the world. You even realize that those around you are far superior to them.

Always remember, never put your pain on other people or rely on them to fix the brokenness in your life. **Maintain faith in the process;** you'll feel better sooner.

Whispers

In the realm of decision-making, heed the whispers of your hesitant heart and the enigmatic stirrings within your being.

Engage in a delicate dance with introspection, for the key to mindful choice lies in that ethereal realm.

Pause, reflect, and let the veils of uncertainty unfurl. Do not cast your life upon the treacherous seas of recklessness, for the journey is arduous and fraught with heartache.

Listen. Be mindful.

At Corridor

Sometimes we sit around and wait for them
to notice us when the opportunity presents itself.

We continue to wait for them to come into our lives,
even though we are aware of
how difficult it will be for them to do so.

We waited because we were afraid we might be disappointed.
But we know that waiting isn't getting us anywhere.

Stand up

We've been knocked down more than once,
but that won't stop us from getting back up again.

Let us use the pain and anguish we've experienced
to push through the difficulties life has thrown at us.

The blood and tears we lose along the way
will be replaced by triumph in the end,
no matter how many times we fall down or
how many tears we shed.

Memory

Even though thinking about us makes me happy
and makes me smile; the truth is that
I was deeply wounded, my heart was deeply broken,
and the scars will never completely heal.
I can't find joy or laughter in anything
except remembering the two of us.
I've been feeling very down ever since you abandoned me.
I know you've found someone who makes you happy,
but I still wish you wouldn't hurt them as you did me.

Simply fight

I know a few people who fight
no matter what life throws at them.

They fight about whether they have issues
with money, family, work, studies, or relationships.

Some people can't handle it and lose themselves,
but I admire people like that
because they are the ones who lose themselves
because they prioritize the fight of family and others
over their own.

I hope we give those we know who are fighting a chance
to speak with us, even if they stumble a few times.

Take heart for those who have lost but are still fighting.

Understand

It's human nature to constantly evaluate oneself in relation to others. Why do they seem to have such a carefree existence?

We don't understand why good people can't escape pain and difficulty in this world. Nonetheless, I came to understand that everyone faces unique challenges. It's possible that those who appear to have it all together to us are actually on the verge of giving up and don't see any reason to carry on living.

I am not

People compliment me because they see that I am able to deal with difficult situations with confidence and assurance. There are a lot of eyes on me because people think I can handle anything that comes my way. One person's final hope is another's greatest source of happiness, and the surplus of happiness I bring to others eventually makes me a need.

I spend a lot of time considering other people's experiences and brainstorming potential solutions to their problems. I know how important empathy is to help others. At night, I feel like I am in prison; I have no strength left, my heart is heavy, and my nerves are worn out.

I let people's circumstances imprison me, believing that tomorrow would bring about yet another conflict in the course of someone's life. A struggle that is not intended to be mine, a struggle against someone else's issue.

I am trapped in a life that has been painted from their own perspective.

My life somehow needs other people who share the same perspective as me.

At the end of the day, I am not a hero.

Challenge

Affection for the unjust.
Have compassion for your oppressor.
Feel affection for your tormentor.
Learn to love your adversary.
Show respect to your enemy.
The best way to avoid being destroyed is to love your destroyer. Affectionately embrace the person who brings you down.
Affection for your shamers.
Be kind to the people who make fun of you when you're feeling down. Affectionately adore them.
Doing so, God will bless you more.

Keep

It was one of the most challenging lessons I had to learn to keep my plans, goals, and life desires to myself rather than share them with others.

It is acceptable to share information with others; however, certain things should not be announced until they have occurred and cannot possibly occur before they have occurred.

Some of your dreams may never come true.

Reason?

There are many ears listening to what you have to say, and there are numerous ways for people to stop you from succeeding.

Keep.

Drains my energy

If these people around me just have negative things to
say about others,
I will lose respect for them.

Those who delight in pointing out the flaws in others'
actions
no longer hold my attention.

I'm losing my admiration for people who can't think of
anything
other than they're only intelligent, good, right.

Having these kinds of people around drains my energy.

Soul

I long for the kind of escape that takes me somewhere quiet and tranquil, where I can finally unwind and feel at ease. I long for time spent secluded from the world, where I can focus solely on God, nature, and myself. My spirit felt as light and free as a cloud at the time. Only the birdsong, the stream's trickle, the smell of jasmine flowers, and the wind's chill reach my skin when I close my eyes. Bring me to that place.

I desperately need it.

Question

Although I am not perfect and frequently make poor decisions, I thank the Lord for blessing me despite my shortcomings and flaws. Do these things belong to me? How valuable I am, and I still feel his favor and grace. He still cares for me, and I can feel his hands guiding me, no matter how often I hurt and ignore him. Is what I enjoy truly deserving of me?

Thank you, Lord!

Mind it

It's okay to shrug off repeated insults from everyone who hates you.
Give them over to God, and keep going.

They act this way because they covet what you have
and are unable to obtain it for themselves.

Remember, you are blessed beyond measure.

Consider how intelligent and strong you are; based on what I've seen, you definitely have more knowledge than anyone else in this room. Now, though, something is blocking your path, and it seems you do not have the power or the will to get rid of it. This time, you are faced with challenging circumstances, you might not know what steps to take, or you are unable to act decisively when faced with adversity. Your resilience appears to be so poor at this moment that you have no idea where to find encouragement or obtain strength, which is really concerning. This time around, it seems you are entirely lost, sinking deeper and deeper into the muck of disappointment and fear. At this point, your knowledge and experience are entirely irrelevant.

I understand your situation because I heard you when you expressed fears. I know you are about to give up. Hold on.

In a moment, I'll make my way over, my friend. We've been in situations like this, and not everyone understands what we're going through.

Better

Is the person you claim to love really that great,
or are you just holding on until someone better comes along?

Do you only hang out with that person
because you hope to get something from them?

Is it love,
or is there simply no one else in your life who can fill that void?

Is it that you're not proud of your relationship
or that you're not in love with the person you're with right now?

It's better to let go of what you don't love so that it can be taken care of by someone who does.

It's ok if you are feeling down today
There are more than seven billion humans living in the world today. Everyone is having trouble and has their own set of problems to solve. We are human, and as such, we are predisposed to experience a wide range of emotions, including sadness. The circumstances surrounding your sadness may be challenging to address, but take comfort in the knowledge that they will eventually pass. Whatever it is that's bringing you down today, know that it, too, shall pass.

It's ok if you are feeling down today
Perhaps today you're feeling anxious or as though there's a pain in your heart. Apparently, the stress of your current environment has left you feeling exhausted and thirsty. It's okay to feel down today. It's hard to imagine, but the pain from your wounds and cuts will likely be gone by tomorrow. Sadness can teach us to value and recognize the sources of our joy.

It's ok if you are feeling down today
It has been a very long day for you. You engaged in conversation with others and brought a smile to their faces. I know it is not easy for you to keep going, but I appreciate your perseverance. You still have mental clouds that obscure your clear thinking and appreciation of life. Just let the unsettling music of the storms and waves continue to wash over you. You did what you could, so now it's time to relax, breathe deeply, and try again tomorrow. Sadness can only be processed and healed if it is acknowledged and expressed.

Embrace

How's your spirit?
Tired? Feel like giving up?
When words fail you, just cry.
To put it another way, every single drop is a source of incredible strength and control.
It's okay if no one cares about your misery;
you need to forge ahead. Get over it;
if no one wants to hear your woes.
Your physical self begs you to stop.
Keep your eyes shut and cry all you want.
Sooner or later,
someone will give you a warm embrace to soothe your troubled spirit.

She

She is a woman with a brave soul,
She is a woman with a happy heart,
She is a woman whom I earnestly pray for,
She is the woman everyone wants to be with,
She is kind,
She is smart,
She is funny,
She is strong,
She is a woman with ambitions,
She is a woman who loves her family,
She is a woman who fears God,
She is talented,
She is captivating,
She is shrewd,
She is sincere,
She is a woman you dearly respect,
She is a woman that gives you comfort,
She is a woman that prays for you,
She is noble,
She is compassionate,
She is resilient,
She is selfless,
She is your mother,
She is the gift of God,
She is a masterpiece.

The powerful weapon

I know you have a hard time making sense of everything that's happening. Maybe you're having a hard time in school, at work, in relationships with loved ones, making ends meet, staying healthy, or juggling all the other responsibilities you feel you have to take care of. Despite going to bed exhausted, you can't seem to fall asleep because your mind keeps racing. At other times, especially when deadlines are approaching, the days will fly by too quickly. You can't enjoy the freedom and contentment you deserve because of all the demands placed on you. To put it simply, I feel you.

When we're feeling anxious, stressed out, or otherwise mentally unsettled, we often turn to the counsel of those close to us for a calming effect. But if we're by ourselves once more, it's as if we've climbed back into the ship of uncertainty, set sail on the waters of our problems and challenges, and are now doomed to drown without any chance of survival because the tranquilizer has worn off. I feel for you.

Stop and take a few deep breaths. Take a look at the things in your immediate surroundings. What makes you think you can get away from everything you're going through? Look, everybody knows that life is tough. It's tough because we live in a world where anything can happen at any time; the future is a murky place where nothing is certain; the present is fraught with anxiety; and everyone is fighting their own battles. That behavior is not excusable on your part. No one is exempting us from this, John C. Maxwell says that the question is not whether you will have problems in life but how you will deal with your problems. Are you worried right now?

You are not alone.

Pray

You could argue that this has a similar effect to that of your friends' advice in that it temporarily relieves distress but ultimately leads to the same feelings of worry, anxiety, and sadness. True, but God intends prayer to have an effect far beyond that of any tranquilizer; the promise of God gives us hope and peace that no drug can match.

Like a soldier, we have access to a potent weapon provided by God: prayer. Some of us either don't pray or struggle to pray because we don't know the what's the proper way or doubt whether it is appropriate. Or perhaps some of us have lost faith in prayer's efficacy, viewing it instead as nothing more than an ancient custom.

To pray is to have power, whether or not we believe it. Never be hypocritical in your prayers to God; do so with complete assurance. We must keep praying and believe that our requests will be answered (Hebrews 4:16, Matthew 6:5–8, Mark 11:24, 1 John 5:14). In addition, we should take Jesus' attitude toward prayer into account, which was one of trust in God's ability but also of submission to his will (as evidenced by his words, "Father, all things are possible for you... Yet not what I will, but what you will") (Mark 14:36).

Call out to God and let him know what you need help with so that he can hear your prayers and see your situation. Be at peace with whatever the outcome of the struggles you are going through may be because this is the will of God, and God is in control of everything that is happening.

Pray.

My mother taught me

My mother taught me many things,
such as how to wash, clean, cook, and dream.
But one thing I learned from her that has shaped who I am today
is how to pray.

These are what I discovered when I prayed;
My soul is at ease, and my mind is clear.
It lifts my spirits and takes my worries away.
When my life is chaotic and out of control, I find peace.

I am hopeful, and prayer directs my steps.
The answer could be yes, no, or wait.
It is still a source of inspiration for me on my journey.
Every day when I wake up, I know everything will be fine.

Even when I fail, I entrust everything to God.
God's will be done, and everything will go as planned.
Prayer is a guiding light in our darkest hours.
Prayer is a powerful tool, and it is the most powerful weapon we have.

Prayer enables us to be steadfast and firm
We are confident that everything is unfolding according to God's will,
My future is no longer vague, there is already an assurance,
Through this, I know that I am not fighting my battle alone.

Is this a match made in heaven?

The wind chimes can be heard making their sound.
The deafening melody that emanated from within her heart
You can feel the sparks like two hearts have started beating.
You and each other are a match made in heaven.
You are perfect, and you are in the best possible place at the right time,

And if you listen closely, you can even hear her heartbeat
Nothing can ever come between you
because you are destined to be one.
The indescribable sense of gratitude and happiness,
She is an angel sent to earth.
Two hearts beating in perfect harmony;
she's made a splash;
she's extraordinary,
She's cut a dash,

Is this a match that was meant to be?
Or it could be just your pleading,
supplication, and dream.
One thing is certain,
and that is that you give heaven everything you have.

Melt my heart

I feel a fluttering in my stomach,
Every time I see you around,
Hair that is both beautiful and fragrant,
Eyes that are both bright and alluring,
Enchanted charm, captivating my heart.
The living *Aphrodite,*

You have such a sweet, angelic voice.
I love listening to how you speak; eloquent.
You have full of wisdom,
You are a walking embodiment of *Athena.*
Your smile is wondrous and fascinates me so much,

One day you passed by;
With a happy smile,
With another guy,
I smiled and gave honor,
To the beautiful and wise *Eris.*

A coin in a fountain

The famous Baroque-style fountain,
Magnificent art from the past,
Trevi Fountain, no other name.

Lonely heart falls in love with you,
Couples celebrated bounty,
I heard the flow of the water,
like a blessing from the heavens.

People were praying and dreaming,
with many dreams and fantasies,
I grabbed a coin and threw it there,
Felt relief when I closed my eyes,
Glad to jump on the bandwagon,
saw the fountain up from the sky.

A person next to me asked me,
"You clutched a coin from your pocket?"
Dreams and fantasies within reach.

The appropriate way of wishing,
In order your wish will come true,
must turn around and face away,
Toss your coin over the shoulder,
Assurance to return to Rome,
and all the wishes, pleas, and dreams,
has a good shot of getting it.

I smiled, paused, and held my heart.
Excited to see it again,
with two hearts brought together
by the heaven who hears my dreams.

Just to remind you.

Let's not make fun of them because they can't handle the trials that lie ahead. Other people simply stop trying. What hardships they endured are unknown to us.

Why not help, motivate, and shed light on their path instead of making fun of them? It's easier to make fun of other people than to examine our own behavior and character. Reflect.

I ran into three familiar faces when I came out of the convenience store. We haven't talked much because we only met at university. The evening was freezing, and my chatty spirit couldn't help but talk to them because I was bored at the time. We laughed and shared some amusing stories during our discussion. Because I was hungry, I decided to end the conversation by asking two questions in each of them.The first question is, "What characteristics or traits of the person do you admire?" And here are their responses:

1. *I like intelligent people; I believe intelligence makes people attractive.*
2. *I admire intelligent people as well. My previous partners have all been intelligent, and I was meant to be with someone intelligent.*
3. *I'm unsure if I'm sapiosexual, but being intelligent is a plus.*

They were all professionals with decent jobs, and yes, I agree that looking for an intelligent person is subjective, and I believe that there are many factors to consider. I then asked, "What makes you dislike someone?" Here are their responses:

1. *I despise people who are arrogant, and I hate people who are intelligent but arrogant.*
2. *I despise people who are only concerned with themselves and those who are manipulative.*
3. *If that person is insensitive and self-centered, I despise them.*

Following the conversation, I learned three things:

1. *Some people do not place a high value on appearance. Yes, appearance is important to some, but being a person is more than that; character is also important.*
2. *If we love someone, we should expect that person to have flaws, and that person's negative attitude can sometimes ruin our feelings for that person.*

3. Finally, there are times when even a brief conversation with someone can be meaningful and productive.

Companion

I'm starting to worry that I'll go crazy without you around every day. In my lowest moments, I am glad to have you by my side. You fortify me when I'm at my weakest, and I replenish you whenever you're depleted. You have heard and read every word I have ever said and know every secret I have ever told. You're always with me, and that's what helps me maintain my sanity. I worry when you're not around. When I hold you, I feel a sense of calm. You can read my thoughts and feelings. You can never be replaced. You connect me to the one I care about. You're a cutting-edge innovation that ranks among the best.

I appreciate having *my phone* as a constant companion.

Purpose

I just wanted to tell you that you are unique and wonderful and that God put you on this earth for a reason. Some people need you to exist, some people need you to be in their lives, and some people find happiness because of you. Remember that you give other people a reason to keep going. This is true; even if you don't recognize it; you were made in a way that pleases God. Realize that you are a masterpiece among many. Recognize that you were made to be exactly who you are because you will soon be heralded as a victorious overcomer.

When you feel like giving up, remind yourself that your worth is independent of what other people think, and know that you have a purpose. Realize that you are a royal, made by the hands of the potter and designed and chosen by the King.

Then I thank God

All of us have been duped by our own hearts at some point.

Sometimes, despite our best intentions and thorough preparation, we end up with the person we like the least.

Not because we are powerless but because our emotions manipulate us.

Despite our best efforts to convince ourselves otherwise, we eventually had to face the person we despise.

How often do we fall for our own deceptions?

As opposed to trying to push someone away, why do we sometimes find ourselves drawn to them like a magnet?

Is there a reason we were brought together instead of being separated?

Sometimes, even if we try to keep our distance from someone, we end up with them as a romantic partner.

Why is it that the person we despise the most is the one who will end up loving us the most at the end of the day? And sometimes we wonder why it is that in our prayers, we thank God that the people we hate the most are the ones who love us the most. This is the case for at least some of us.

Whisper

You've repeatedly demonstrated it, but the expected outcome remains elusive. Count the number of times you've attempted and failed to accomplish your goal.

How many times have you attempted to reach something, but no matter how hard you try, you can't get there? Sometimes you feel like giving up, but you will continue to attempt new things and take chances anyway. This, you told yourself in silence, is the best you can do.

You were about to give up, but then....

someone whispered in your ear, hugged you, and encouraged you, saying, *"Fight, believe it; you will soon reach whatever you want; just be patient; I will accompany you."* All of the sudden, your heart is filled with hope.

Then your strength returns and you heard this....

“you are with me”.

Let's approach this with an open mind and heart. Even if you may be on the verge of giving up, the things you pray for are still within reach. Meditate.

Your life may occasionally be chaotic, but it is not always
as messy as you would believe.

Meditate and trust God.

Close your eyes and declare that "God is with me".
We face numerous life difficulties, anxieties, and
worries,
and we even feel abandoned and rejected.

Meditate and trust God.

You are not abandoned, I can assure you of that; you
only need to experience these emotions in order to carry
out God's purpose and plan for your life.

Don't doubt it.

It's never too late to make a fresh start in realizing your dreams.

Remember that as long as you are breathing and have the ability to move, you may accomplish your goals. Your plans may occasionally succeed, you may become lost in your course, or it may be difficult for you to recover. I know you can move heaven and earth to achieve your ambition, so pick up the pieces you left on the ground and gather all of your strength.

It's never too late to start with a clean slate in achieving your goals in life.

Me too; I just regained the strength I needed to continue.
I look forward to what lies ahead.

ABOUT THE AUTHOR

Nathaniel E. Quimada had a challenging and eventful upbringing in Claveria, Misamis Oriental. Whose parents had to toil daily on the farm to make ends meet. His tough upbringing inspired him to aim high and go the extra mile, demonstrating to those around him that anything is possible with hard work, faith, and the support of loved ones.

He received his Bachelor of Science in Environmental Engineering from Misamis Oriental State College of Agriculture and Technology (now known as the University of Science and Technology of the Southern Philippines or USTP). He completed his graduate studies at the University of the Philippines- Diliman and graduated with a Master of Science in Environmental Engineering.

Currently, he is the Executive Assistant to the Vice Chancellor for Academic Affairs and the In-Charge of the Innovation and Technology Solutions Office at USTP-Claveria. Also, the College of Engineering and Technology counts him among its faculty.

He began writing multiple literary works due to his experiences. Despite his apprehension about properly establishing his thoughts and sentence construction, he accepted the challenge because he knew that the meaning of each line he expressed was more important.

www.ingramcontent.com/pod-product-compliance
Lightning Source LLC
LaVergne TN
LVHW010117170826
845678LV00012B/2444

9786218397408